Pivot Points

Pivot Points and Portals

A Poetry Conversation
by

Caroline Johnstone & Karen Mooney

First published 2024 by The Hedgehog Poetry Press

Published in the UK by
The Hedgehog Poetry Press
Coppack House, 5
Churchill Avenue
Clevedon
BS21 6QW
www.hedgehogpress.co.uk

ISBN: 978-1-916830-01-1

9 8 7 6 5 4 3 2 1
A CIP Catalogue record for this book is available from the British Library.

Pivot Points and Portals was typeset using the Dyslexie font to make it more
accessible.

Welcome to our poetry conversation.

We dedicate it to all those who prefer a good old-fashioned exchange, preferably in person and with a cup of something - something that seems even more important since Covid.

So, for those who like to chat, those who need to be heard and those who so often cannot find the words — feel free to dip into ours, where you might find that a conversation is a pivot point in life or a portal into another.

Decisions, Decisions

Moments of choice are eternal precipices

tsunamis of dropped chance stitches

golden threads of sliding door stories

doors to prison

portals to Narnia

Contents

TO THE EDGE

Where houses and the warmth
of lighted windows end –
when you go beyond
the voices and the noise
that punctures your thoughts
go beyond even the silence of graveyards
where mortality is frozen in time –

there will be nothing to see
but darkness

or what the moon might
pick out for you –

the half-collapsed barn door
an owl that swoops in shadows
the wild things that watch, waiting.

COLOURING IN

im My Uncle, Samuel Hewitt & Samuel Nevin

Displaced from the family farm,
that you, as the eldest son,
should have been running,
living at a crossroads,
in a little cottage called 'The Corner',
on the boundary of the family farm.

Paralysed by Polio,
yet
your garden; an artist's palette
of aubretia, carnations, and geraniums;
where the birds always sang.
Mum said you created it from slips,
dragging yourself on an old sack to tend it.

I recall you framed in the doorway,
propped up on wooden crutches,
their leather-padded tops pushing
your arms out, making you look
broader, stronger ...

I was probably only five or six
when I saw you back in the farmhouse,
lying in a big wooden box
at the top of the stairs, grey.

A greyscale memory
I held in fear for many years,
haunting my childhood mind
after seeing you in Sunday dress,
wooden framed, frozen in time.

Until I see a same-named guitar playing
lookalike gracing the stage of social media,
tugging my memories with each riff,
colour-washing my recollections,
erasing the fear.

He, too, dragged himself around —
to gigs whilst desperately ill,
but his music lives on
and I see you, like your garden,
edged with life and colour.

THE WALLED GARDEN AT DUMFRIES HOUSE

It goes without saying: weeds not allowed, no signs needed.

Here, red brick walls
copings askew as old mortar crumbles
match the gravel that creeps into your shoes.
They shelter straight rows and hedges
edged with life and colour
from winds whipped up from the river below.

Paved paths are softened with formal planting
unscented roses, trellised honeysuckle
the delphiniums that stand guard at the back.

Painted Victorian seats discourage contemplation.

Black metal gates hide warm compost heaps, beehives,
the invitational warmth of the gardeners hut; a place to rest
from hothouse heat and cold frames.

Outside, oblivious, the wild things concentrate
on living well. Grasses sway in winds
they've learned to bend in,
nod to neighbours —
golden buttercups, red clover, pink tinged daisies,
brambles, proud purple thistles.

BORROWED SEASONS

April tears up the Almanac,
refusing to cast off winter's clothes.
Squatting in doorways, she inhospitably
blocks the admission of seedtime.

Ragged, malnourished, begging
for sustenance yet obstinate,
denying invitational warmth
of extended light on old bones.

Her debt to the seasons is overdue.
Will they underwrite her mulish
denial of time, compensate us for
keeping her company, as she lags behind?

STAKES IN A WASTELAND

I fall in love with each
abandoned house I notice;
want to fill them up
with love and light // and life again,
rescue them from // oblivion,
neglect,
        their falling apart.

Here, windowless eyes
observe a small grove of trees
once planted for shelter, firewood —
Roots, undisguised,
deep in the river's edge
are stakes in a // wasteland
        declaring it home.

There, by the lintel,
scattered with sheep droppings,
the door sags // begging for sustenance //
hangs on resolutely
by the one hinge left.

Flaked paint tells the same
pride and joy story,
        asks why everyone left.

A SONNET FOR JIM – I THINK OF YOU AS A TREE

im Jim Adams

Ringed with experience, furrowed with care,
with all of our names carved close to your heart
we danced around you in pleasure, shared
fears as you offered branches laden with art.

Your photos captured dreams etched in the skies,
you shared music, like birdsong, it always
hit the right note. Roots, and accent, undisguised,
stretched along the river's edge, hoping for ways

to slow the flow whilst you drank in the view.
Anxiously, we all took a pew to hope and pray
for so much, we couldn't say lest you knew
how we feared what the swelling banks conveyed.

Uprooted, we, at sea; you: homeward bound,
to be held forever within a gentle sound.

THE HOUSES I DREW AS A CHILD

were always the same. Substantial
like Sunday dinner with pudding,
yet light and delicate as silk with their solitary tree,
branches laden with art, the small white
picket fence, a winding path
to the strong front door of a country cottage,
that chimney ready for the first offering
of the hearth.

This was my perfect house
and like my best laid plans
and the flimsy perfection I reached for
through the small irritations of life
it lies in tatters and lies hanging in the air
like cobwebs, ghosts of wedding veils.

WAITING FOR DAD TO COME HOME

The streetlight traced mum's dignified poise,
flickering, candle-like, on the glass china cabinet
as she searched for dad's car headlights
through a yawn of gates.

Standing in the bay window of the good room,
she scrutinised the night, fears ticking louder
with each chime on the mantelpiece.
Mum recalled that my brother once said,
"don't worry, mum, they'll tell you if he's dead."

We didn't have a phone, but who
would you call in the darkest hours
of the *whatever you say, say nothing* days?

Years later, we learned
that he had been sent to the riots.
He never talked about what happened,
only that he hated to see good food wasted
when he found himself being pelted
with tinned soup and fruit.

Having known the hunger and thrift
of being reared in the thirties,
this was beyond his understanding.

His response was to fill the pockets
of his great black overcoat with tins
and bring them home to us —
His own small act of resistance.

So tinned tomato soup sometimes
replaced mum's homemade variety,
and for afters, something with custard.
often tinned peaches.
But it wasn't worth the waiting.

SIXTH FORM

Do you remember
how the ripples of the Hunger Strike
made it to every village
and on to South Belfast, where they rustled
through the silence of deserted streets
the silent screams
from inside our heads
and a sixth form commute through the division
of morning prayers and school uniform colours
and whatever you say, say nothing days

how the school was emptied of noise
and of younger children
as tension crackled through streets hung in the air
like cordite,
how we'd laugh in explosions
of held-in breath as we'd look
over our shoulder at the car

we'd manage to tiptoe past
without triggering a bomb

how youthful our hope was
in flak jackets of burned plastic
metal peppered with ribbons
of flesh and bones.

REVOLVING DOORS

Trapped

we'll try again

inside

one more time

wanting to shout

before we try again

lacking the courage

to stop the door

to stick out a foot

to block the next revolution

find a way out

mute the screams

inside our heads

that speak volumes

whilst nothing is said

Trapped

A LIFE WITH HOLES IN IT

Grief comes, demanding our attention,
throws open the doors to darkness
rooms crowded with averted eyes,
that speak volumes
whilst nothing is said
trapped

With time and tiny steps,
we try to adjust to a life
with holes in it, turn our backs
on our loss yet meet it round each corner
in songs, a date, each time we go
to share a story,
for grief remembers itself
in winds that moan in their uprooting of trees
in the void and the veil
of deep winter.

THE PROBLEM WITH DUST

Grief is weary in the waiting
and gathering of itself and the dust to dust
of a solemn parade of flat-footed undertakers.

We can try to clean it away
turn our backs
on our loss yet meet it round each corner
try to hide from it like a hermit
but it will venture out,
visit old haunts
curl itself under doors
creep past closed curtains
seep through any crevice
as if it needed to announce
its presence over and over again
so you pour it on to your
corn flakes,
stir into your tea like ashes.

IN SEARCH OF LIGHT

im Jim Adams

In between treatments, you venture out;
visit old haunts, catch a movie, visit a gallery,
hold family near whilst showing no fear;
full of fight.

In between treatments, you venture out;
cross the Irish Sea with your children
and grandchild, hoping that her first steps
will be taken at the Giant's Causeway.
A visit home with family, to family,
you catch up with old friends,
crafting memories in plain sight.

In between treatments, you venture out;
buy another guitar, eleven, the final count.
Camera in hand, you capture images
of flowers, looking up, you take one of a tree
which you send to me together with family news
and updates from hospital reviews.
And, as with every exchange —
I study it for light.

THREADBARE

We stood in the margins of light
looking out at the bright garden
from the darkness of the scullery door,
drank in the strong rows
as if we had a camera in hand
to capture summer fruit and wallflowers

I was five, maybe six and I remember
how my great grandmother's apron —
threadbare, patterned with flowers -
wrapped around her good clothes,
reached to the laces of her sturdy
brown shoes, how her right hand
was deep in the pocket jostling
the essentials - a clothes peg,
clean handkerchief, peppermints -
and her left hand was on the back
of my head like a hiding place,
a sword, a blessing.

MARRAM GRASS

Let me be your hiding place,
your sword, your climb hold.
Let me break your fall.
Let me protect you,
bind us together,
let me frame your view.
Let me slow these shifting times,
holding memories,
let me.

WHEN I HEARD THE TOWNLANDS OF COUNTY DOWN WOULD DISAPPEAR

Let me slow these shifting times;
let me tell you these things
so you too can remember

that the blarge of ice-flows in retreat
were impatient fingers that cowped
drumlins to shape them
blazing like your blindness

to a reality like pregnant bellies
caressed by sun, soft rains,
            to be spaces of holy grun, unseen worlds –

that rivers like veins
bear ancient stories to lakes
that gather in a bewilderment of tears
for their loss

Leggygowan / Glassdrumman
Drumalig / Lisdalgen.

blarge •heavy blow cowped •spilled
grun •ground •townland ancient divisions of land that are
unique to Ireland

DISTANCE

You drove us to the water tower,
hoping
that watching the inky heavens
through the one-touch opening
sunroof of your sleek, fastback coupé
would lure an unsteady star.

Standing hairs stretched,
ready to cushion my fall
till the cosmos cast
cloudy apprehension
of the sky falling in.

Grasping at cool night air,
the prize slips through fists
of impatient fingers
before dawn intercedes,
blazing like your blindness
to a reality that you
were light-years away.

BLACK HOLES

At first, rose-tinted eyes just saw the brilliance
of two unsteady stars colliding.

Shaken, rearranged, we were blinded
to any other world existing -
glued together, like shadows haunting each other.

In the cold light of day, cracks appeared
in the darkness of the sky falling in as we

imploded like supernovas,
fell apart at the seams, a singularity of loss
and black holes.

· E C L I P S E ·
· brave   like the moon ·
· I   stood   in   your   light ·
· felt   the   heat   of   you ·
· then   moved away   lest   I too ·
· got burned - that   saintly   halo ·
· proved   to be nothing more ·
· than   the   cold ·
· light of day   ·

THE ONE THING WORSE THAN PAIN

The one thing worse than pain
is feeling nothing at all.

There, in a liminal space,
the weight of our world washes over us.
We float in formaldehyde,
micro-bead soups of other people's
good intentions, prayers, our own

sense of despair that nothing changes.

We observe the world in silence, grey clouds
hanging in same old skies, no remote control
to change them though anything is better
than being glued down by fear.

Like winter seeds, crack open
to surrender, slow kisses of possibilities.
May you be brave like the moon.

May today be a triumph of life over flatlines
where you listen to your life, let its heartbeat
hold you together, let you limbo under
whatever stops you living, open the gate.

ACKNOWLEDGEMENTS

Thanks are due to the following publications in which some of the poems, or versions of them, were first published: Paragraph Planet, Live Encounters Poetry & Writing, Lothlorien and Acumen.
Special thanks to Mark Davidson, Editor of The Hedgehog Poetry Press, for the opportunity to have these poems published and for his ongoing support and encouragement.